The Spindle Whorl

A Story and Activity Book
For Ages 10–12

Including
A Teaching Guide

by
Nan McNutt

Central Coast Salish Cover Art by
Susan Point

Illustrations by
Roger Fernandes

WestWinds Press®

Text © MMXI by Nan McNutt

Credit for illustrations is as follows:
front cover and page 21—Susan Point;
title page, tools throughout—Nan McNutt;
pages 4, 6, 8, 9, 10 (boy carving), 11, 12, 14, 15,
17–20, 22, 24–28, 30, 33, 42, 43, 45–56—Roger Fernandes;
pages 7, 10 (maul and wedge), 16, 44—Kim J. Kaino.

All rights reserved. No part of this book may be reproduced or
transmitted in any form or by any means, electronic or mechanical,
including photocopying, recording, or by any information storage
and retrieval system, without written permission of the publisher.

First printing 2011

Library of Congress Control Number: 2011938958
Softbound ISBN: 978-0-88240-762-3

Book compilation © MMXI by
WestWinds Press®
An imprint of Graphic Arts Books
P.O. Box 56118
Portland, OR 97238-6118
(503) 254-5591

Cover Design: Elizabeth Watson
Interior Design: Jean Andrews

Printed in the United States of America

Thank you weavers and spinners of the coast.
Your whorls sing strong songs.

Crisca Bierwart	Vi Hilbert	Carolyn Marr
Barbara Brotherton	Elaine Humphrey	Jennifer McCord
Randy Buschard	Bill Holm	Astrida Onat
Jill Campbell	Bill James	Laurel Sercombe
Keith Carlson	Fran James	Patricia Shaw
Roy Carlson	Jeanie James	Wayne Suttles
Mark Edert	Dorothey Kennedy	Nile Thompson
Gina Grant	Michael Kew	Roberta Trahan
Larry Grant	Terrence Loychuy	Cindy Williamson

Jo Voss, Steve Chavez, Rick Lemberg, AE #2 Decatur Elementary School,
Seattle, Washington—3rd, 4th, and 5th grades, 1998
Karen Holm, The Evergreen School, Shoreline, Washington—4th and 8th grades, 1998
Tamara Stone, Nancy Meyer, Beth Schneidler, Wolfle Elementary School,
Kingston, Washington—3rd and 4th grades, 2008
Helen Kraft, Margaret Mead Elementary School, Sammamish, Washington—4th grade, 2008
Kara Herber, St. Matthew School, Seattle, Washington—4th grade, 2008

Thank you for sharing your knowledge and time so that
others might experience and understand.
We raise our hands to you!

Welcome! The story in this book will take you on a journey into the distant past. You arrive 500 years ago at the mouth of the Fraser River in Canada, where Central Coast Salish people have lived for generations. The Fraser River is the longest river in Canada at 1,375 kilometers (854 miles) long, and runs from the northeast to the southwest of British Columbia.

The original language spoken by the people living on Fraser River delta is called hən̓q̓əmin̓əm̓, and it is very old. As you read, try using the following "word key" to learn the way the hən̓q̓əmin̓əm̓ words sound. In this language, capital letters are not used for names, places, or at the beginning of sentences; however, in this book, for clarity, we have used capital letters for proper names.

- hən̓q̓əmin̓əm̓ (**hun** cu me num) traditional language of people living on the lower Fraser River delta—hən̓ sounds like "hundred" but ends with a little catch in the throat, q̓ə as in "cup," mi as in "me," n̓əm̓ sounds like "number."
- səl̓səl̓əye (sul sul **ye**) 'Spinning Woman'—səl̓ rhymes with "pull" with a little catch in the throat at the end, repeated, əye sounds like the beginning of "yet." [səl̓ət (sul **oh**) is the root word which means to spin something (such as wool).]
- səl̓səl̓tən (sul sul **ton**) 'spindle whorl'—səl̓ rhymes with "pull" with a little catch in the throat at the end, repeated, tən rhymes with "son."
- stal̓əw̓ (**sto** low) big river' (referring to the Fraser)—sta sounds like "stop" with a catch in the throat, l̓əw̓ is like "low" but with a catch in the throat.

Central Coast Salish Region

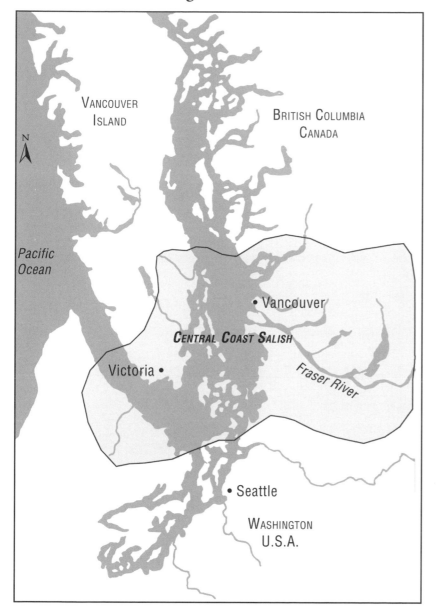

Pacific Northwest Coast Region

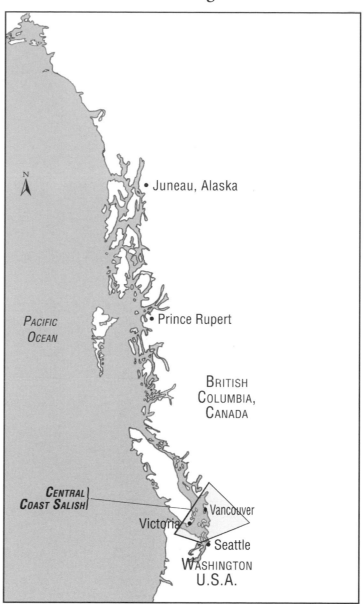

Səl̓səl̓əye (sul sul **ye**) stops spinning. She listens to the sounds of rushing water along the big river, stal̓əẁ (**sto** low), and people sleeping in the enormous old longhouse.

It is long before anyone in the house should be up, but Səl̓səl̓əye is too excited to do anything but spin.

From the sleeping platform she shares with her little sister, Səl̓səl̓əye looks around the cedar-plank longhouse. She hopes her spindle whorl isn't making any noise.

All of her father's family—her parents, grandmother, aunts, uncles, and cousins—seem to be asleep on the platforms that line the sides of their home.

"I've got to finish spinning your fur into balls of yarn," she whispers to her woolly white dog. "I only have a few weeks left. The yarn must be ready to give away at Father's feast, along with other gifts we have made for our relatives from upriver."

As she whispers, she winds the yarn she has just spun around the wool ball resting on the whorl.

She continues whispering. "It's tradition to host the other side of the family. They'll bring us lots of food from upriver, like dried salmon and elk, and we'll give them a lot of our foods that they don't get, like seal and halibut. And, of course, we will be giving gifts, because Father is hosting the feast. A proper host shows generosity this way."

Səl̓səl̓əye (sul sul **ye**) rolls the shaft up her leg. This force turns the round spindle whorl faster and faster, spinning the wool into yarn. As she finishes spinning the wool that she has with her, she pushes the whorl up toward the narrow end of the shaft. The whorl slides up the end, and with it comes the ball of yarn she has just spun.

"There!" she says. "One more ball of yarn is done! It would be fun to learn to spin on a big whorl."

There is nothing more enjoyable to Səl̓səl̓əye than spinning wool on a səl̓səl̓tən (sul sul **ton**). Her older brother carved it and gave it to her as a gift at her Naming Ceremony the year before. Her father had hosted a large party for her, and Grandmother had announced her adult name, Səl̓səl̓əye. It had been her great-aunt's name, and it means "Spinning Woman."

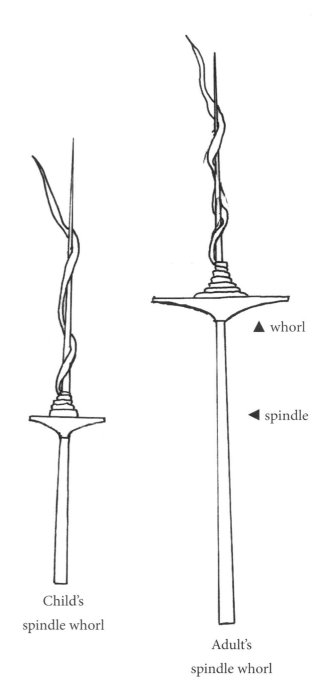

▲ whorl

◀ spindle

Child's
spindle whorl

Adult's
spindle whorl

Səl̓səl̓əye hears tapping sounds outside. "Did you hear anything, Curly Tail?" she whispers to her close companion. He looks up at her and yawns. Concerned, she looks again across the hard dirt floor toward the end of the longhouse. Her older brother's sleeping platform is empty.

She gently jiggles her little sister awake. "I think I hear Brother outside on the beach," Səl̓səl̓əye whispers. "Let's go see what he's up to."

Both girls quietly adjust their cedar-bark
skirts and capes and tiptoe by the fire tender fast
asleep by the hearth.

Waves gently lap against the shore as gray light
marks the separation between water and sky. Brother is
nowhere on the beach. Then they hear tapping sounds that
lead them to the side of the house.

"What do you think he is doing?" whispers Little Sister.
Both girls peer around the side of the house.

9

Their older brother sits on a log, carving a new whorl with his beaver-tooth knife.

Beside him rests the spindle shaft and his tool kit. Inside it are a maul and wedge for splitting cedar house planks to replace the old ones.

"What are you doing, carving so early in the morning?" Səɬsəɬəye asks her older brother. "You can hardly see where your knife is going!"

"Look who's talking," he quickly replies. "Did I hear a mouse spinning earlier this morning?"

They all laugh together.

"Are you making a gift, too?" asks Little Sister.

Brother nods. "Our gifts will show others that we are a good family. Everyone will know we are willing to share what we have." He holds up the whorl. "How do you think Uncle's wife will like it?"

Little Sister moves closer to look at the design. With a pointed finger she traces the outline of a large bird. "What kind of bird is that?" she asks.

Her brother grins. "What do you think it might be?"

Səɫsəɫəye smiles. She remembers the time she asked Grandmother about the images on her large old səɫsəɫtən (sul sul **ton**). Grandmother's only reply was, "What do you think it might be?"

"It's a bird flying," Little Sister guesses. "But I also see the head of a fish. I know! I know! Maybe it's a . . ."

Suddenly the dogs begin to whine and whimper.

"The dogs! We'd better get going," says Səɫsəɫəye "We're supposed to wash and feed them early so that Mother and Auntie can clip off their woolly hair."

Səɫsəɫəye and her sister hurry to the dog pens behind the longhouse. Their cousin comes out of the longhouse to join them. She and Səɫsəɫəye are the same age and are always spinning and weaving together with the older women.

"Will you and Auntie spin the dog's hair into yarn?" Little Sister asks as she trots alongside her older sister and cousin.

"Yes," Səɫsəɫəye replies. "And then Mother will weave the yarn into beautiful white robes. It is important that we have robes to give away at the feast. They show that we are good and prosperous people." She gives her little sister a grin. "Who knows? Maybe someday you will spin and weave, too."

Little Sister beams back at her.

The girls spread out cattail mats on the ground, where they will cut the dogs' clean fur. They hurry off to the pens to feed the dogs cooked salmon. "Father says that salmon and deer meat make the dogs' fur really thick and shiny," says Səl̓səl̓əye's little sister.

"Yes, that's true," replies Səl̓səl̓əye. "That's why our dog-hair blankets are prized by other villagers along the stal̓əw̓, the river."

Cousin has brought with her balls of baked white clay to clean the dogs. Səl̓səl̓əye leans toward an older dog and whispers as she combs, "Old One, are you ready to get rid of all that long hair?"

The dog tosses its head with an excited little bark. Səl̓səl̓əye smiles, knowing that having their heavy fur cut will be a welcome relief to every dog. Soon Grandmother and Auntie come to help. One by one the dogs' long, woolly hair is cut off with sharp mussel-shell knives. Səl̓səl̓əye loves to separate out the long, fluffy fur from the short, coarse wool. She imagines herself spinning with it on a larger whorl one day.

"Səl̓səl̓əye," her cousin nudges her, "what are you thinking about? You look as though you're in another place."

12

Embarrassed, Səɬsəɬəye giggles. "I was just wondering if Uncle's new wife spins with white mountain goat wool. Their wool is much easier to spin, but it is hard to get here, along the river."

"You are always thinking about wool," Cousin teases. "Last night in your sleep you were spinning the tassels of your blanket with your fingers!"

It takes most of the day to shear all the dogs, and by the time they are done they have a mountain of fur to spin.

"You girls have a lot of work ahead of you," says Grandmother with a smile.

* * * * *

At last, the day of the feast has arrived. Səɬsəɬəye and her cousin busy themselves helping the older women cook and place food in large wooden bowls. They smell the salmon, sturgeon, and halibut, along with the seal, sea lion, deer, and elk, roasting on the open fires. All the delicious food that the women of her family have made to share with their guests reminds Səɬsəɬəye of the basketful of yarn she will present to Uncle's new wife. "I really hope she likes it," she thinks, anxious to do her part to show her family's skill and prosperity.

Young boys playing near the water spot the canoes coming around the bend in the river.

"They're coming! They're coming!" they shout, running toward the village.

Səɬsəɬəye's family hurries to clean up and dress in the finely woven dog-hair robes Mother and Grandmother had made.

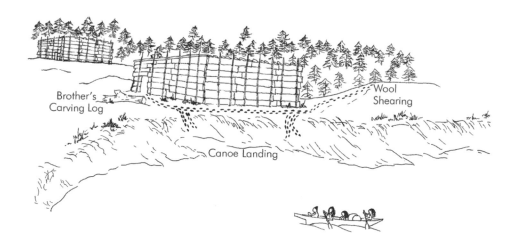

Brother's
Carving Log

Wool
Shearing

Canoe Landing

As the canoes get closer, Səɫsəɫəye and her entire family can see Uncle, their mother's brother, in the lead canoe. He stands wrapped in a white mountain goat robe. Right behind him, a young woman, also wearing a mountain goat robe, sits on bundles of goods.

As the lead canoe nears the shore Uncle raises his arm as a gesture to honor those who are there to greet them. His deep voice rings out across the inlet waters, announcing their arrival to the family gathering on the beach. Səɫsəɫəye joins her family as they line the water and beat a quick rhythm on their drums and sing back to the visitors.

"Look, there's Uncle! And that must be his new wife!" says Little Sister.

Səɫsəɫəye gazes at the young woman who is only a few years older than she is.

"She is pretty, isn't she? I wonder what village she came from before she got married. Her parents arranged her marriage, just like Mother and Father will arrange a marriage for me. And you, too. That is our custom, so we will have proper husbands."

"I'm not ready to get married!" says Little Sister stubbornly.

"Neither am I. But someday, when we are older, we will be ready," says Səɫsəɫəye.

"Do you think Uncle's new wife spins or weaves mountain goat wool?"

"Why don't you ask her?" says Little Sister.

Səɫsəɫəye nods.

"Maybe one day I will get to spin and weave an entire blanket made just from mountain goat wool."

Uncle addresses his relatives and the other villagers. In the lead canoe, his voice is deep and clear. "Greetings to my brother-in-law's family, and to the other good people of this village. We come to honor you. We have traveled a long way down the staĺəẃ (**sto** low). We ask permission to come ashore, to the house of my brother-in-law!"

"Welcome, yes, welcome!" Father's voice booms like a drum. He is dressed in the finest dog-hair robe. Red, brown, and black geometric patterns trim its edges. "We are honored to welcome you to our village. You bring cheer to us all. Come ashore, come ashore!"

Səĺsəĺəye moves up beside Grandmother, facing the canoes that have come such a long distance. The drums beat rapidly, and a chorus of voices begins to sing an ancestral welcome song. Səĺsəĺəye sings with them. Low and high voices join together, and the melody of the song rises and falls over the steady rhythm. She watches as her brother and the other young men rush into the water to help the visitors to the beach.

"Come into the longhouse," Father invites his brother-in-law, family, and other guests from the village. "We have prepared food for you all."

Once the guests are inside the longhouse, they are made comfortable on platforms that will be their home for the next few days. By the light of the three fires set up in the middle of the house, Səĺsəĺəye and the other women of her family begin bringing in the large bowls of meats and fish. The parade of food continues with seaweed and salmon egg soup, baked camas and clover roots, and the finest fish oil. The feast is about to begin.

The wonderful smells of dinner fill the house and excite everyone. As Sə́lsəlʼəye and the other women from her father's house serve the guests, they hear the upriver people commenting on the food.

"Oh my, look at all the candlefish oil! I can't wait to dip the tender clams into it."

"Did you see the elk meat and the seal? How delicious!"

Sə́lsəlʼəye feels very proud. She knows their food is appreciated and that their guests will continue to hold her father's family in high regard.

Father takes his place at the center of the floor, close to the honored guests. He seems tall and regal as he stands before the entire family. Then, with a deep and powerful voice, he begins.

"Welcome to this house, dear relatives. It is a great honor that you have traveled such a long distance to be here. We have not seen you for some time, and it gives us such pleasure to spend this time with you. I only hope that we can honor you as much as you have honored us."

People lift their arms in gratitude, and then excitedly begin eating from the large bowls of food.

Then Uncle calls upon the family from the upriver village. They present to Father and the family many baskets and boxes filled with huckleberries, bear, deer, fresh elk and mountain goat meat, and bundles of dried smoked salmon.

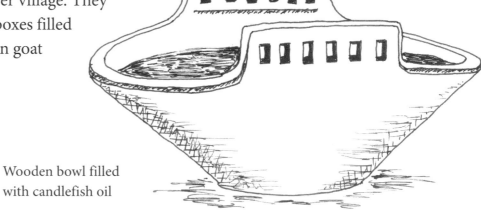

Wooden bowl filled with candlefish oil

It is late when Father and Mother bring out their gifts.

Brother helps hand out robes and blankets that Mother and Auntie have woven. There are also bone pendants, stone beads, and maple wood canoe paddles that Father and Brother have carved.

Finally, Brother presents his special gift. He holds his newly carved səl̕səl̕tən (sul sul **ton**) up high for all to see. Uncle admires the quality of his nephew's carving.

Then Father calls upon Səl̕səl̕əye. She cautiously steps out from behind her brother before a house full of guests. She knows that she is not allowed to speak. Her father will talk about her good qualities and her wonderful skill with spinning wool into yarn. She takes a deep breath, straightens her back just as she has seen her father do many times, and steps up beside him.

"My dear people!" Father's voice is rich and deliberate. "Beside me stands Səl̕səl̕əye, who has received the name of my dear departed aunt, given to this young woman at her naming ceremony last year. Səl̕səl̕əye wants to welcome all of you who have traveled so far to come to this home. It is an honor for her to have you here."

Səl̕səl̕əye breathes deeply as she listens to Father's words. Her arm is wrapped tightly around her basket filled with yarn.

17

"In honor of her uncle and his new wife, Səİsəİəye has spun a basket full of yarn for you. She wishes to express her gratitude to you dear people."

"Thank you for your generosity." says Uncle. "These are wonderful gifts that both you and your brother have made. These not only show us your accomplishments, but they also let us know that your family has brought you up to honor and respect others. Thank you."

In appreciation, Uncle's wife holds up one ball of dog-hair yarn for all the people to see. Səİsəİəye and her brother gratefully raise their hands to honor their uncle's words.

As Səİsəİəye returns to the platform with her mother and little sister, she smiles when she thinks of the pride she saw in her father's eyes.

A week later, when the guests have returned to their home laden with gifts, Səɫsəɫəye is still glowing from her family's wonderful party. So many people shook her hand, and Uncle's new wife thanked her for the beautiful gifts.

"Səɫsəɫəye," calls Grandmother, who is seated on a bench, "Come and sit beside me." Mother and Auntie continue spinning and weaving.

As Səɫsəɫəye kneels beside Grandmother, she notices Grandmother's large old səɫsəɫtən in her hands.

"I have something important to say," Grandmother begins. "You have honored all the members of our family. Your gift to Uncle and his wife of finely spun wool shows how you have lived up to your adult name. It is a name to which you bring honor."

"I am getting too old to spin with this big səɫsəɫtən as I once did. You will spin with it now."

Səɫsəɫəye is too surprised to speak, and for a moment there is silence.

"Grandmother," asks Little Sister, "what is carved on the səÍsəÍtən?"

Grandmother strokes her youngest granddaughter's long, black hair. "Tell me child, what do you think it might be?"

"I see a face, and it's like the face is speaking or singing." She pauses. "Like when Father sings or makes an important speech. And I see fish that are coming out from the face. Maybe they are salmon being presented in an important way."

"Yes, my precious little granddaughter. The image in the səÍsəÍtən is what you see, what you understand, and what you experience."

Sə̓Ísə̓Íəye and Grandmother smile at one another. "Sə̓Ísə̓Íəye, your great-great-grandfather carved this səÍsəÍtən for me when I came of age and was given my adult name," says Grandmother. "Now you will spin with it, until someday, as a grandmother, you, too, will hand it down."

20

► Grandmother's
Whorl

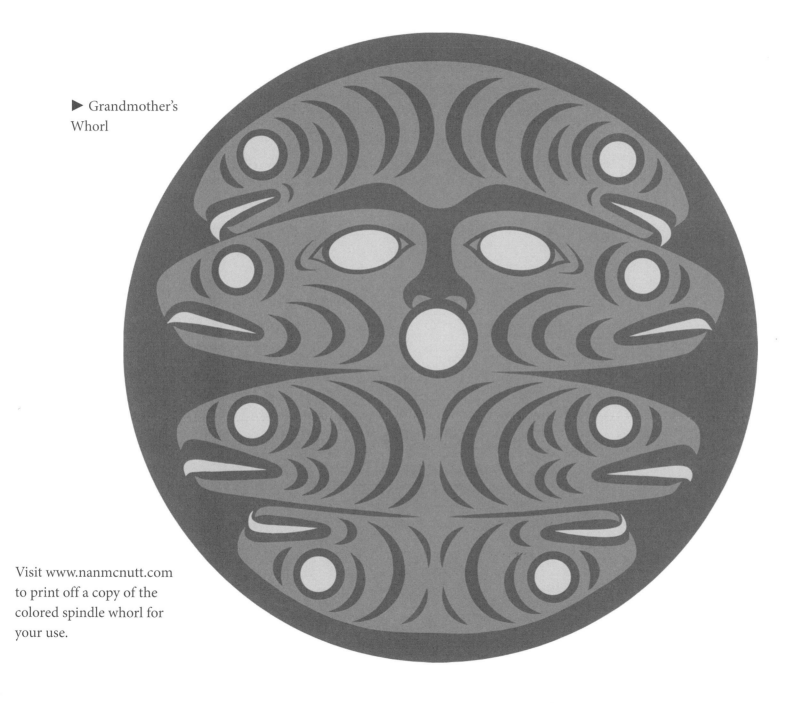

Visit www.nanmcnutt.com
to print off a copy of the
colored spindle whorl for
your use.

Take Wings and Fly!

The carved image on the spindle whorl Brother made for his new aunt is similar to that on a whorl at the Smithsonian Institution in Washington, D.C. Traditionally, men carved whorls, but today women carve, too. Susan Point, a well-known artist, lives on the Musqueam Reserve in Vancouver, B.C., Canada. She uses traditional images for her inspiration.

First, carvers create an outline of the image. Next, they carve away the area surrounding the bird. This carved-out area is called negative space.

Question to think about:
If the space around the bird is negative, where is the positive space?

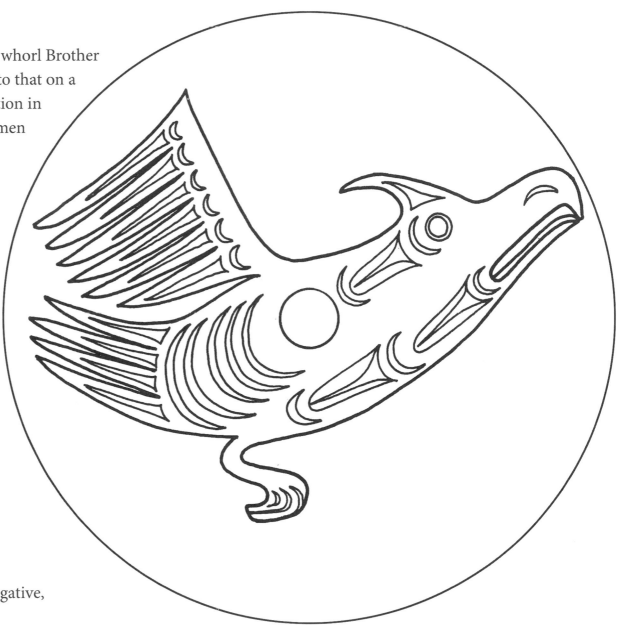

Explore the Importance of Space

The carver was very clever in making this bird look as if it is flying.
It is an illusion created by both the negative space and the positive space.

You need:

photocopy of whorl design
on page 22

crayon

pencil

ruler

paper

1

Color the negative space around the bird.

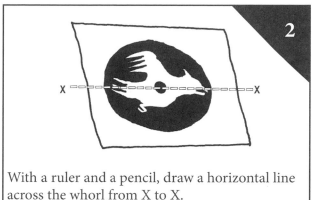

2

With a ruler and a pencil, draw a horizontal line across the whorl from X to X.

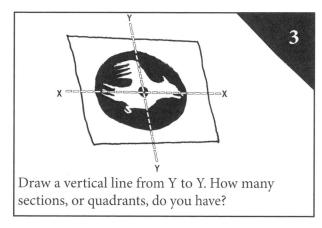

3

Draw a vertical line from Y to Y. How many sections, or quadrants, do you have?

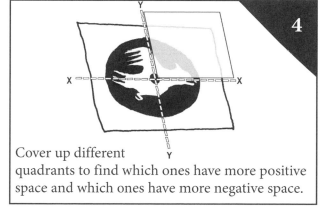

4

Cover up different quadrants to find which ones have more positive space and which ones have more negative space.

Questions to think about:

Which quadrant(s) helps create the illusion of flight? How?

Inside Scoop

Special shapes are carved inside the bird design.
The cuts that are scooped out become negative space.

Practice making the special shapes used in Central Coast Salish art.

You need:

pencil

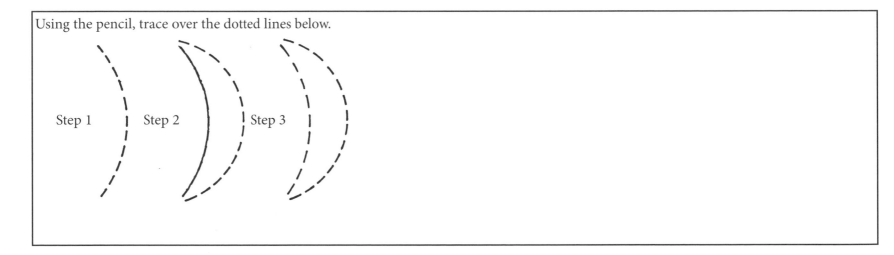

Using the pencil, trace over the dotted lines below.

Step 1   Step 2   Step 3

This shape is called a crescent.

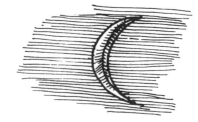

Below is a second shape used in Central Coast Salish art.
Susan Point calls this shape a wedge.

Illustration of carved wedge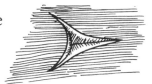

You need:

pencil

Trace over the dotted lines in each step below.

1

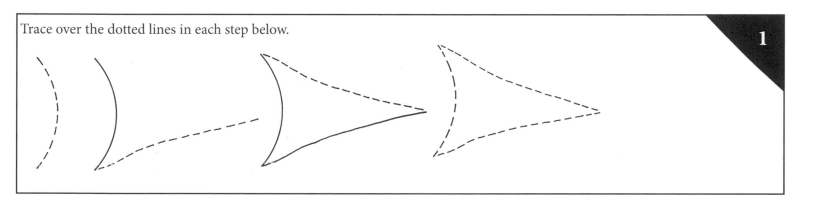

Draw three more wedges on your own.

2

Repeating Patterns

The carvers who created this whorl used repeating patterns of crescents and wedges to add the illusion of movement to their designs. Draw the patterns below on a sheet of paper.

You need:

pencil

paper

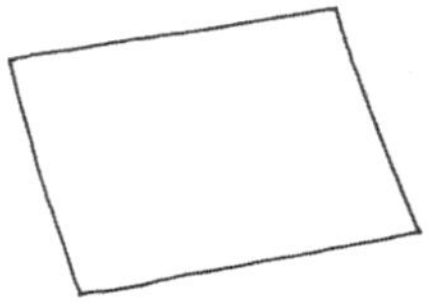

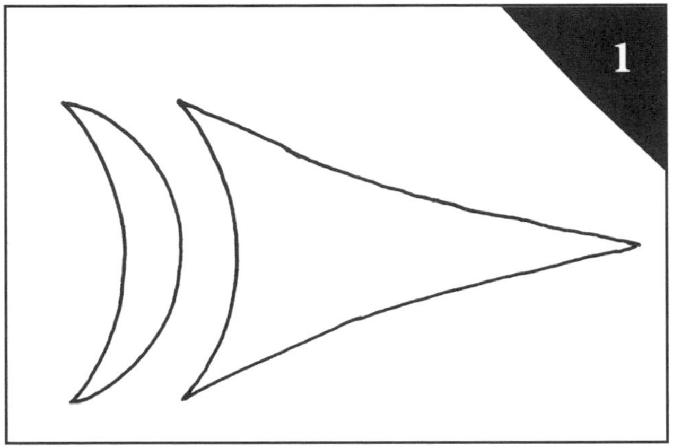

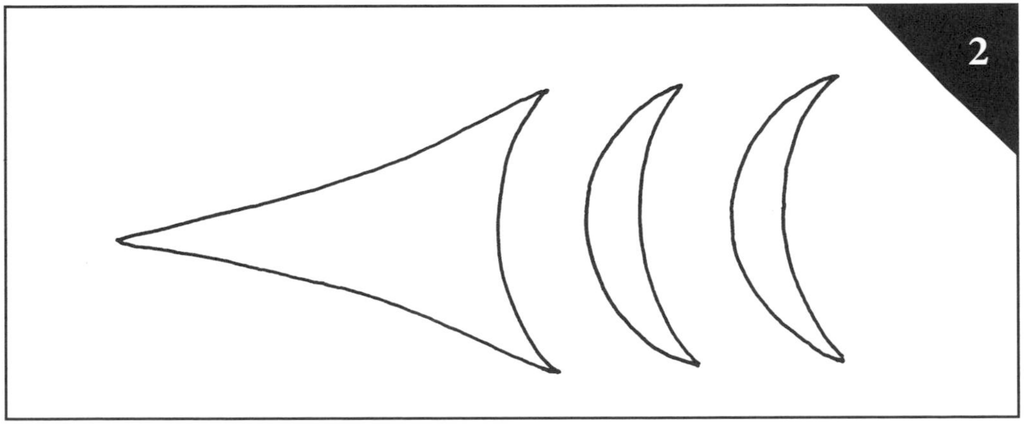

Question to think about:

Can you see the movement created by these shapes?

Draw an arrow below each of your patterns to show the direction you think it is going.

Swimming Salmon

To create parts of an animal's body and give them an illusion of movement, artists carve patterns on the positive surface of the illustration of an animal or being. Using crescents and wedges, draw patterns on the fish to make it look like it is swimming.

You need:

scissors

colored pencil

copy of fish illustration on next page.

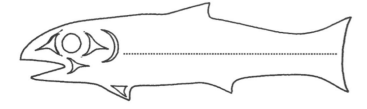

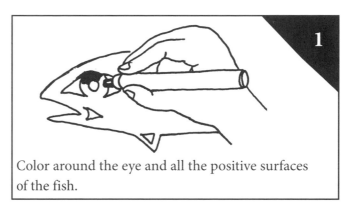

Color around the eye and all the positive surfaces of the fish.

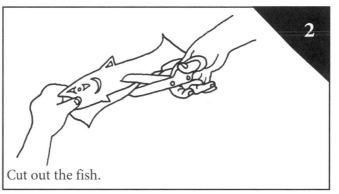

Cut out the fish.

Swimming Salmon (continued)

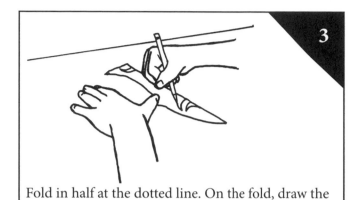

3

Fold in half at the dotted line. On the fold, draw the top half of a crescent and wedge pattern.

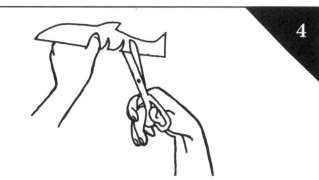

4

Keeping the fish folded, cut out the half wedges and crescents. Unfold fish.

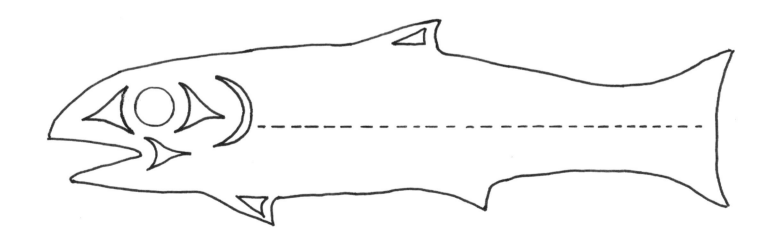

Finish Drawing This Animal

This is part of the image on a spindle whorl that is now at the Smithsonian Institution. Using the drawing skills you have learned, finish the animal on the whorl.

You need:

pencil

Can He Catch His Tail?

This is how the original artist carved the spindle whorl. Perhaps your animal's body is different, but it probably has crescents and wedges like the ones here.

Watch the design twirl around and around as the animal catches his tail.

You need:

copy of this whorl design

colored pencil

scissors

frisbee

Color the positive space, then cut out the whorl. Tape it inside a frisbee and spin it to see what happens!

The Splitting Wedge

Central Coast Salish artists carve one other shape. Try your skill at a splitting wedge!

You need:

pencil

Using a pencil, trace over the dotted lines. **1**

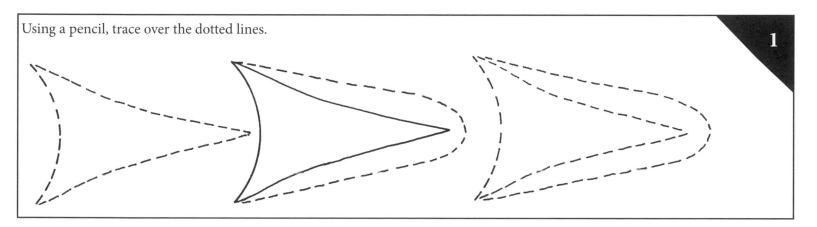

Draw three more splitting wedges. **2**

What Do You Think It Might Be?

Among Central Coast Salish people, images in whorls hold special meaning.
These images are not named; they are left for each person to interpret in his or her own way.

You need:

pencil

colored pencil

Using a pencil, continue the split wedge pattern across the body of the animal.
Color the positive surface with a colored pencil.

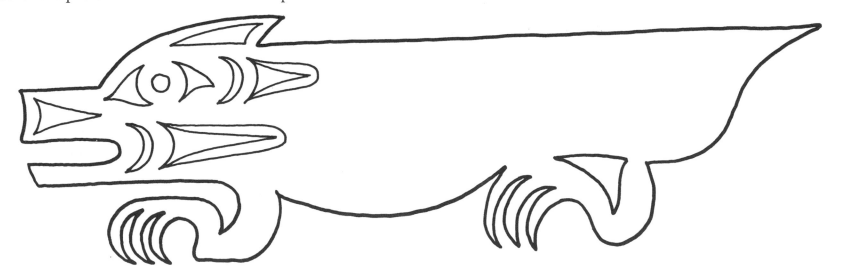

The image in the whorl is what you see, what you understand, and what you experience.
—Grandmother

Here is a similar image carved into an old whorl. It is housed at the Smithsonian Institution in Washington, D.C.

It is an eye dazzler!

Do you see any similarities to the animal on page 32?

You need:

colored pencil

Color the positive surface of the animal, but not the negative surface.

Questions to think about:
Ask a partner to watch your eyes as you follow the split wedge patterns. Does he or she notice your eye twitching around? Why do you think your eye is twitching?

Make a Whorl

You need:

two paper plates

poster board or
old file folders

glue

scissors

paper clips

canning jar

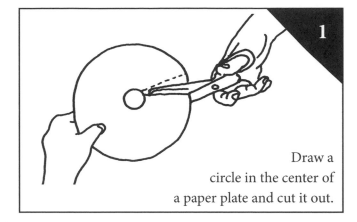

Draw a circle in the center of a paper plate and cut it out.

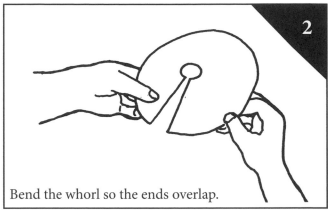

Bend the whorl so the ends overlap.

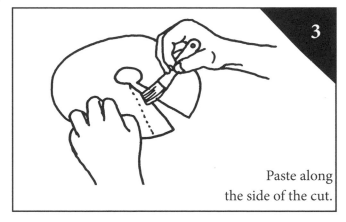

Paste along the side of the cut.

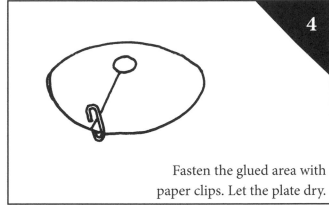

Fasten the glued area with paper clips. Let the plate dry.

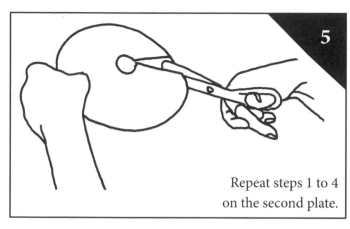

Repeat steps 1 to 4 on the second plate.

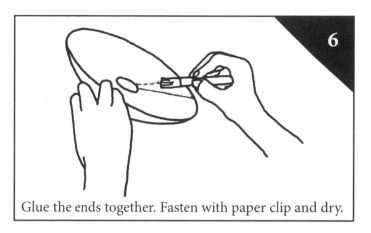

Glue the ends together. Fasten with paper clip and dry.

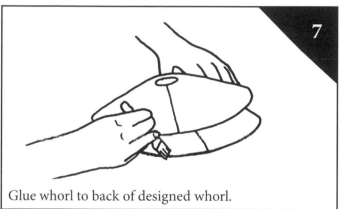

Glue whorl to back of designed whorl.

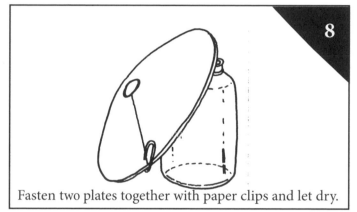

Fasten two plates together with paper clips and let dry.

Question to think about:

What design will you draw on your whorl?

Roll the Spindle Shaft

You need:

tape

butcher paper
(18"x 24")

paper whorl you
made on page 34

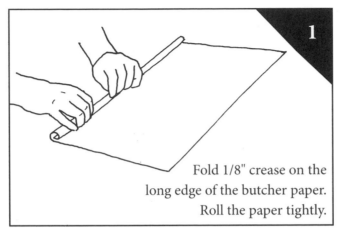

Fold 1/8" crease on the
long edge of the butcher paper.
Roll the paper tightly.

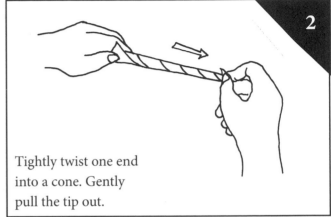

Tightly twist one end
into a cone. Gently
pull the tip out.

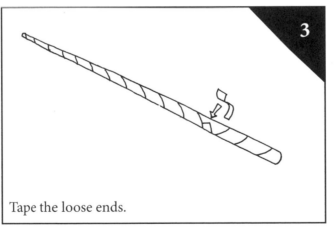

Tape the loose ends.

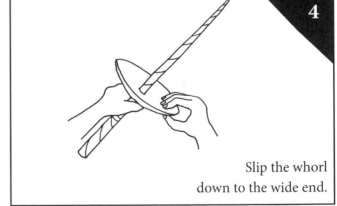

Slip the whorl
down to the wide end.

This illustration represents a tiny stone whorl that is 4$\frac{1}{2}$ inches in diameter. It was found at the Milliken Site along the Fraser River Canyon and is about five hundred years old. To make the whorl, the carver used water and fine sandstone to grind the shape and lines. To create the wedge forms, the stone was pecked with a harder, pointed stone.

You need:

your eyes

List three or more observations about this ancient whorl that remind you of the other whorls in this book.

1. _____

2. _____

3. _____

4. _____

5. _____

6. _____

Animal Impressions

Many Central Coast Salish carvers use the positive and negative spaces in their whorl designs to print the image on paper. Give it a try! Draw and then make a print of your own animal design following the instructions below.

You need:

newspaper to cover table

pencil

2 pieces foam core (4" x 6") or clean foam meat tray

paper

table knife

all-purpose glue

tempura paint

your finger or art roller

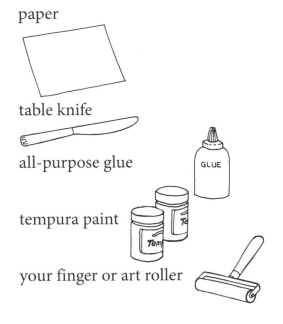

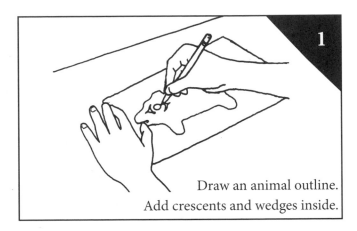

Draw an animal outline.
Add crescents and wedges inside.

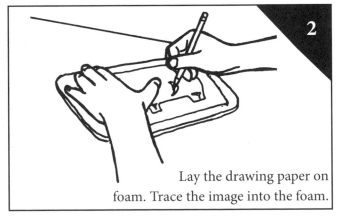

Lay the drawing paper on foam. Trace the image into the foam.

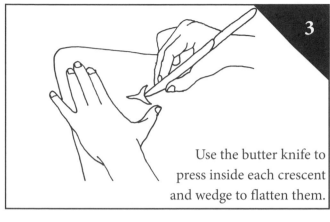

Use the butter knife to press inside each crescent and wedge to flatten them.

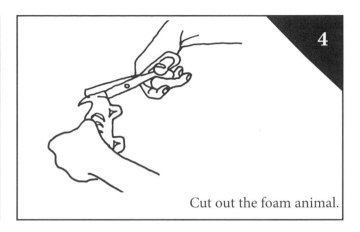

Cut out the foam animal.

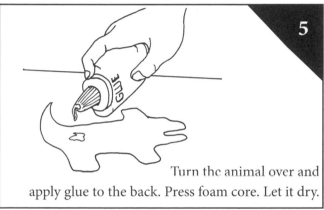

Turn the animal over and apply glue to the back. Press foam core. Let it dry.

Apply paint to the positive surface but not in the flattened parts.

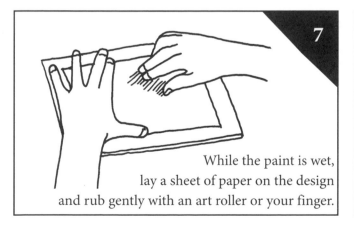

While the paint is wet, lay a sheet of paper on the design and rub gently with an art roller or your finger.

Pull the paper off slowly, and let dry.

Teaching Guide

Spinning and weaving were, and are still, a part of Native people's lives all along the Northwest Coast. Involvement in both of these activities helps nurture and sustain traditional values in Native life. Spindles were used all along the Northwest Coast, but only the Central Coast Salish people who lived along the rivers and inland waters of what is today northwest Washington and southwest British Columbia carved images into their whorls.

The Spindle Whorl shows the importance of whorls and their carvings to the Central Coast Salish people.

It is one book in a five-part series on Northwest Coast Native American art and culture: *The Button Blanket* (grades K–2), *The Cedar Plank Mask* (grades 3–4), *The Spindle Whorl* (grades 3–5), *The Twined Basket* (grades 5–6), and *The Bentwood Box* (grades 5–6). Each book uses its title object to share the different art forms practiced by various Native American cultures along the Pacific Northwest coastline.

For more information about Central Coast Salish people and their art, the following reference materials will be very helpful.

Select Bibliography

Gustafson, Paula. *Salish Weaving.* Vancouver, B.C.: Douglas and McIntyre; Seattle: University of Washington Press, 1980.

Hill-Tout, Charles, *The Salish People.* Ed. Ralph Maud. Vols. 1-5. Vancouver, B.C.: Douglas and McIntyre, 1978.

Holm, Bill, *Spirit and Ancestor.* Seattle: Burke Museum; Vancouver, B.C.: Douglas and McIntyre, 1987.

Johnson, Elizabeth L., and Kathryn Bernick. *Hands of Our Ancestors: the Revival of Salish Weaving at Musqueam.* Museum Notes No. 16. Vancouver, B.C.: University of British Columbia, 1986.

Point, Susan. *Susan Point: Coast Salish Artists.* Vancouver, B.C.: Douglas and McIntyre, 2000.

Suttles, Wayne, *Coast Salish Essays,* Vancouver, B.C.: Talonbooks, 1987.

Websites: www.nanmcnutt.com; www.susanpoint.com/home.htm

More about the Story

Native American children today are as modern as any other kids. They wear the latest fashions, play soccer and basketball, and read books that inspire them. And yet Native American children inherit a culture that is thousands of years old. While the traditional values and practices have changed through time, they still provide a strong link to the past.

Today Native American children are learning to speak and read their traditional languages. Some of the sounds and letters/symbols are similar to English, some are similar to French or other languages, and some are totally different. In this story your students or children will be learning new sounds and letters/symbols. Have them look at the introduction to a dictionary. There they will find a pronunciation key for many letters/symbols used throughout the world. This will help them become more familiar with the varying sounds and alphabets of the world's many languages.

Cultural change is an important issue that affect us all. Most cultures are in constant flux, especially in today's world. It can be difficult for people living in a diverse mainstream society to recognize their individual culture. To explore different cultures with your students or children, you may want to include a parallel study where each child researches his or her own culture and how it has changed over time. Using one object or custom from his or her culture/family helps to narrow the research.

Stages of Life—The Story

The Spindle Whorl portrays Central Coast Salish women in many stages of life before the coming of Euro-Americans in the 1700s. The central character, Səɬsəɬəye, is a young woman who is about 10–12 years of age and from a well-to-do family. Her family has been able to afford both the expense of a Naming Ceremony for her and her brother, and a feast for the distribution of foods between the father's and mother's families.

Səɬsəɬəye has proven herself as a hard and conscientious worker, particularly as a fine spinner. At the time of this story, she has already received a guardian spirit helper and spiritual vision that will guide and help her throughout her life. These were important elements in becoming an adult. She may have had her first menses and received training in the proper etiquette of an eligible woman.

Girls of Little Sister's age were still emotionally expressive, curious, and playful, but they learned how to attend to tasks alongside the older women. One such task was helping to care for very small children and babies.

Typical of babies from the Central Coast Salish upper class, the baby shown here is cradled in a basket with a headboard, and her head is gently bound with cedar bark to slope the forehead. All children of upper- and middle-class families were cradled in this way, their faces a broad appearance. This was not only a sign of beauty but also a sign of upper- and middle-class men and women.

Uncle's wife is older than Səɫsəɫəye, perhaps sixteen years of age. She wears a robe made from mountain goat wool, which shows she is also from an upper-class family. Marriages were set up by both sets of parents, who were most interested in increasing the economic ties with one another, which provided economic diversity and continued status.

At the time of this story, Səɫsəɫəye's parents may have already made arrangements for her future husband. While in modern culture we might view arranged marriages in a negative light, this process was welcome in Səɫsəɫəye's time. The knowledge that her parents were helping in the preparation of her adult life was reassuring.

The feast in the story is a time for exchanging food and gifts between in-laws and others invited to the party. This kind of party celebrated the political alliance between the two sides who supported each other. The leaders and members from the host house were seen as having increased their prestige. However, the guest family brought gifts of food, which kept them in good if not equal standing. With the exchange of goods and foods, both sides demonstrated their commitment to one another, which brought economic stability for the future of their children.

At the end of the story, Grandmother portrays the last stage of a Central Coast Salish woman's life by giving an heirloom to Səɫsəɫəye and a gift of wisdom to Little Sister. While women her age would continue to carry out their daily tasks in their extended family's home as long as they could, their utmost concern lay in guiding their grandchildren's proper behavior, maintaining their status, encouraging their achievements, and teaching them about their family lineage and spiritual knowledge.

Dogs, Mountain Goats, and Wool

Creating a story that takes place before the coming of Euro-Americans requires the blending of scant and sometimes conflicting references derived from oral stories and written literature. However, it is clear from ethnographic and archaeological accounts that the wool dog was a small- to medium-size curly tailed dog, bred exclusively for its woolly hair.

While an exact date of the origin of the wool dog is not yet known, the first archaeological evidence of a domesticated breed thought to be the small animals dates back three thousand years. These dogs were kept isolated from other dogs so that interbreeding would not occur. The wool dogs were always attended by women and were the property of women. They were fed special diets of salmon and meat, sometimes lived in the homes, and were sheared like sheep twice a year for their highly prized fur.

By the 1800s overwhelming numbers of Native Americans had died from the diseases brought with the vast influx of Euro-Americans. With such devastation to the people, and in turn, the culture, the wool dog could not be properly cared for, and interbreeding eventually eliminated the pure wool dog. Today what remains of this old Central Coast Salish dog is one dog pelt at the Smithsonian Institution, yarn, blankets, and stories.

The use of mountain goat wool lasted longer and is still common in some places today. At the time of this story, mountain goats *(Oreamnos americanus)* lived in the Coastal Mountains, where they were hunted for meat and wool. Their wool could be easily gathered where it caught on the low branches of wild bushes around where they grazed.

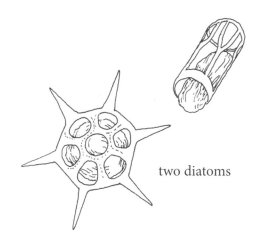

two diatoms

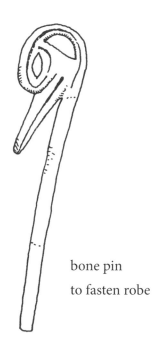

bone pin
to fasten robe

The coat of the wool dog is different from that of the mountain goat. The wool dog had long, soft hair as well as short, coarse hair. The mountain goat's coat consists of long, coarse guard hairs and short, soft hair. Women pulled out as many course hairs as possible, leaving the rest to be spun.

The wool, whether from dogs or mountain goats, needed to be cleaned. The primary ingredient for this task was white clay, or diatomaceous earth. Diatomaceous earth is found in different parts of the continent where plate tectonics have uplifted ancient sea deposits. These deposits contain the diatom's siliceous skeleton, which effectively traps small particles. Today, crushed diatoms are used as cleaning filters for rocket fuel and swimming pools, and even as an insect repellant in gardens. The Central Coast Salish people discovered and used the excellent cleaning qualities of diatomaceous earth to "dry clean" their wool and wool robes.

Introduction to Central Coast Salish Art

The earliest archaeological findings of Central Coast Salish art on decorated stone, bone, and antler fragments date to around 4,500 years ago. Central Coast Salish artists began using crescents, circles, ovals, and wedge-shaped gouges to delineate the various parts of animals they carved. These design elements are demonstrated in the two artifacts illustrated here and on pages 45 and 46: a bone pin and a brow band fragment.

The shapes that Brother used to carve his whorl were the crescent, the wedge, and the split wedge. The traditional names for these cuts and forms no longer exist or perhaps never did exist.

In the late 1800s Euro-Americans began collecting spindle whorls. Others were found in archaeological excavations, but due to poor preservation only those made of stone remain.

Most wooden whorls are made from maple, but whorls can also be made from bone and sometimes stone. Most of the wooden whorls were plain, but those with carvings reveal a wide range of carving skills. This suggests that both highly skilled artisans and amateurs decorated whorls.

The Central Coast Salish people consider their personal powers a private matter and rarely talk or publically display them to others. This is very different from the northern Northwest Coast Indians who publicly display their family or clan designs in the form of crests. Among the Central Coast Salish people, depictions, if any, are limited to symbolic designs or generic representations of humanoid, animal, insect, and plant forms.

Combs like the one shown below (circa 1800) were not only used as personal objects but also to comb and cleanse animal wool.

It is thought that spindle whorls were decorated because of their spiritual importance in the cleansing process that the wool went through as it was transformed into yarn, and finally into a robe that represented power.

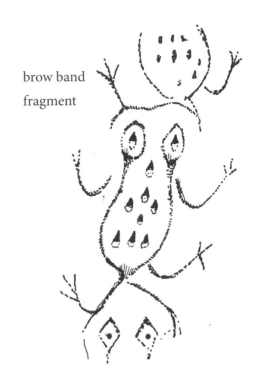

brow band fragment

Design Your Own Whorl

Creating an original design on a whorl will challenge students but can be quite rewarding. If they have never worked with a compass, allow time for them to explore the instrument's use and practice making circles.

You need:

- compass with pencil
- 2 color pencils (a dark and a light shade of the same color)
- ruler
- poster board

Directions:

Drawing the Whorl

1. Review the steps for making a whorl on pages 34–36.
2. Hand out the compasses and poster board. Have students set each compass at $3\frac{1}{2}$" for the radius of the whorl.
3. Draw a circle by placing the compass's point in the center of the desired space and then turning the compass so the pencil outlines a circle. This is the outer edge of the spindle whorl.

4. Set the compass at $\frac{1}{4}$" and center the compass point in the first hole. Draw a circle. This is the center hole of the whorl that will be used to insert the shaft of the spindle.
5. With a ruler, draw a solid line from the center hole to the outer edge of the whorl; this is the radius.
6. Draw a second radius line, beginning $\frac{1}{8}$" inch outside the first radius on the center hole. Make this second line dotted.
7. Now have the children cut the whorl along the outer edge.
8. Then cut along the solid radius line to the center.
9. Cut out the center circle. Leave the dotted radius line intact. Glue the cut edge to the dotted line, making a convex form.

Designing the Whorl

1. Have the students create a design on the whorl. The design on the newly cut whorl should be left open for each student's imagination.
2. Color the design with two colored pencils, a dark and a light shade of the same color, which will give the feeling of a carved relief and an illusion of depth. The darker color is best for the negative surface.

Assembling the Whorl

1. With the compass and poster board, have students make a second whorl, following the instructions on page 47. (This whorl will have no art design, as it is glued to the "bowl" of the whorl with a design.)
2. Following the directions, glue the two whorls together into one complete whorl. Follow the instructions on page 36 to assemble a spindle shaft.

Spinning with Your Whorl

Background Information

Spinning wool does not require a spindle, shaft, or whorl. In fact, a lot of spinning was, and still is, done by rolling wool on a person's thigh. The mechanical advantage of the spindle whorl is that the weight of the whorl and its inertia help make the yarn more even.

Spindle whorls vary in size up and down the Northwest Coast. The whorls made by the northern tribes are approximately $2^{1}/_{2}$ inches to 3 inches in diameter. They are sometimes concave but can also be flat. The accompanying spindle shafts average about sixteen inches in length. None of these whorls have designs.

Whorls of the more southern tribes, the Coast Salish, Makah, and Nuu-Chah-Nulth, vary widely, ranging from about eight to twelve inches in diameter. Adornment is limited to the larger whorls, though many of those are plain. The shafts for the large whorls are four feet long.

Additional substances were sometimes added to extend the materials being spun. Fluff from cattail heads or fireweed, as well as duck down, were added to supplement the wool and add to its insulating value.

Today only a few people use spindles. Most home spinning is done on a mechanized spinner, fashioned from an old sewing machine and driven by a foot pedal.

While you may have never spun wool, consider taking the time to do the following activity. You cannot imagine how rewarding it will be for you and your children or students. Don't be too surprised when you find out that many children do not know that clothing is made from threads or yarns! You may even want them to pull threads from a piece of cloth to help them better understand how fabric is made.

Spinning can be difficult, so it is a good idea to try it on your own before teaching it to others. You can follow the instructions on the following pages to learn how to demonstrate spinning while the children are doing the art activities. (You can sit on a stool for better viewing.) This will give the children the advantage of knowing what the spindle whorl is and how it works.

You need:

- 1 oz of carded wool
- a sharp pair of scissors
- magnifying lens

- 1/2 oz. of uncarded wool
- scraps of yarn, twine, and rope

Introduction

Discuss with your children or students the traditional ways Northwest Coast Native American children and apprentices learned from masters. First children and apprentices observed for a long time without questions. By watching every moment and every step of the process, they learned to imitate the actions of the master. They would practice their skills later, on their own. Finally, when their efforts were successful, they worked alongside the master.

Activities

Wool. What is it?

1. Divide the raw wool among the children. Allow time for them to examine the wool.
2. Hand out the magnifying lens and ask the students to look at the wool under a lens.

3. They should draw what they see and include descriptive words.
4. Ask what would happen if they washed the wool, or pulled wool out as far as they could? Have the children record ideas that can be tried out. Share these and record the results on a class chart.

Unwinding Yarn, Twine, and Rope

1. Have the children handle several samples of scrap yarn, twine, and rope. Each child should select one sample to work with.
2. Draw and label the direction of the twist. (S-twists angle to the right; Z-twists angle to the left.)
3. Now ask the children to take their sample and untwist it.
4. With the samples in front of them, lead a discussion about their observations.
5. Have the children draw and label their observations of the untwisted wool.
6. Now have them twist the samples back together.
7. Discuss how they would make thread, yarn, rope and twine.

Advanced Activities Spinning Yarn

Making a Roving

1. Unroll the carded wool and separate out a section of fibers approximately 12" long and ¼" around.
2. Gently pull on the ends of the fibers so that you lengthen and thin the entirety to approximately 24" long. Don't pull too hard or the fibers will fall apart.
3. Lay the bunch of fibers on the top of your thigh and roll them down your thigh. What you have just made is called a roving. This process of rolling helps make the fibers more compact and holds them together as they are spun into yarn.

NOTE: Graphics in the following sections relate to the directions; i.e., written directive #2, see illustration #2.

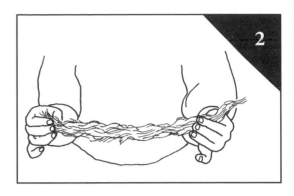

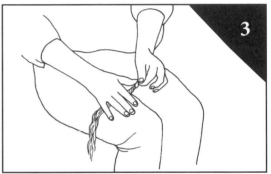

Rolling the Shaft

1. Lay the spindle across the top of your lap. If you are right handed, the thick end of the spindle should rest on your right thigh. Left-handed people should do the opposite.
2. Identify the parts of the spindle: the shaft and the whorl.
3. Make sure your legs are spread apart enough so that the whorl fits between them.

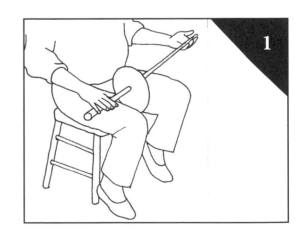

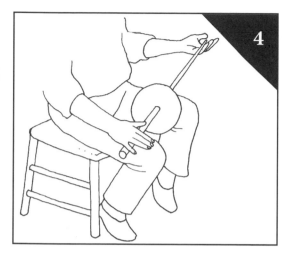

4. Lightly place your right hand palm down on the base of the spindle, which is resting on your right thigh.

5. With open palm, use your left hand to gently lift the small end of the shaft.

6. With your right palm, press across the shaft and gently roll it up your right thigh. Keep your palm on the shaft at all times.

7. While you are rolling with your right hand, your left hand cups and steadies the tip of the shaft so that it does not move.

8. Once the base of the shaft reaches the top of your thigh, lift it up and place it back down with your right hand to roll it up again.

9. Practice this rolling until you feel comfortable and in control of the spindle whorl.

Attaching Roving to Spindle

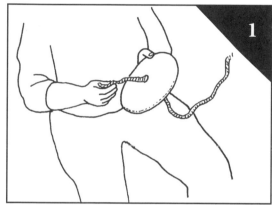

1. Remove the whorl so that you can insert the end of the roving into the center hole of the whorl.

2. With the roving inside the center hole, gently pull the whorl down the shaft until it fits snuggly and the roving is secured tightly.

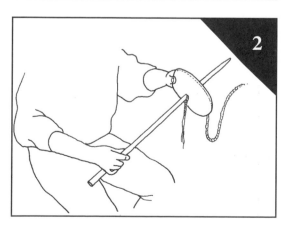

Spinning Yarn

1. Lay the spindle back on your lap.
2. With your left hand, pick up the roving between your thumb and index finger, pinching it tightly.
3. Rest the small end of the shaft in your left palm. Cup your hand to secure the tip.
4. Place your right hand on the base of the shaft, which is resting on your right thigh, and roll the shaft up your leg. This twists and spins the roving into yarn.
5. While spinning, keep the roving tightly pinched between your left thumb and finger and hold it straight out from the end of the shaft.
6. Continue this spinning action while you tightly "pinch" the roving.
7. Stop the spinning action and look at the twists that have gathered in front of your pinch.
8. Slowly and gently loosen your pinch, without letting go of the roving, and slide your thumb and index finger away from you and up the roving.
9. Watch the twists travel up the roving. When they stop, apply your pinch once more.

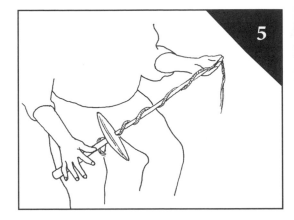

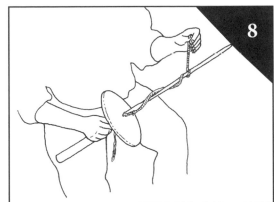

Wrapping Yarn into a Ball

When the yarn becomes too long to continue spinning, you are ready to ball the yarn around the spindle. Continue holding your "pinch" through these steps.

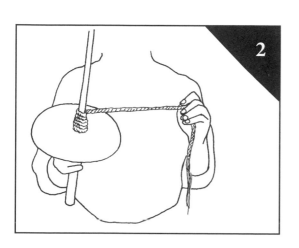

1. With your hands, yarn, and spindle in the spinning position, use your left hand to pull the yarn away from the tip of the shaft toward you at a 90-degree angle.
2. With your right hand, lift the spindle and hold it upright. Then turn the shaft. As you do this, the yarn will wrap around the shaft, balling up in the dish of your whorl.
3. Keep turning the shaft until your left hand (still pinching the end of the spun yarn) meets the tip of the shaft.
4. If at any time you need to stop spinning, roll the end of the spun wool (yarn) around the ball and press it to the spun wool. It will attach itself to the spun yarn.

Adding New Roving

1. When you've finished spinning the first roving, leave the ball of yarn in the dish of the whorl and make a new roving.
2. Pinch the new roving to the end of the newly spun yarn.
3. Continue spinning, allowing the twists to build up by your "pinch."
4. Loosen and slide your finger and thumb up the roving, allowing the twists to continue making new yarn.
5. Continue spinning, adding new roving and winding the yarn around the shaft.
6. If at any time you wish to stop spinning, wind all the yarn around the shaft. The yarn fibers will catch on one another and hold the end of the yarn in place.
7. To remove the yarn from the shaft, simply slip the balled yarn off the shaft and store in a sack or basket. If you are using a paper whorl, lift the whorl to loosen the end of the original roving, held between the shaft and the inner hole, and simply lift the yarn off the whorl.

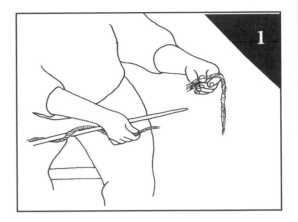

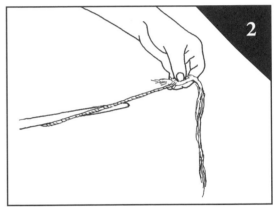

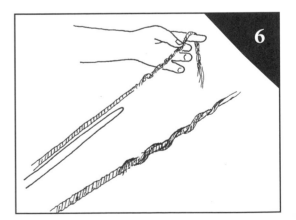

Artists of *The Spindle Whorl*

Susan Point was born in 1952 and grew up in a family that actively celebrated Central Coast Salish heritage. This formed a solid basis for Susan's artwork, which relies heavily on cultural artifacts such as Central Coast Salish spindle whorls. Susan's work now graces the National Museum of the American Indian in Washington, D.C. One set of her full-size house poles welcomes visitors at the Vancouver International Airport, while others decorate public buildings and corporate developments on both sides of the Canada/U.S.A. border. She was elected to the Royal Canadian Academy of Arts and has been presented with a National Aboriginal Achievement Award in recognition of her work as well as her influence in honoring Coast Salish art.

Roger Fernandes is a Native American artist and educator, who delights both children and adults with his storytelling and the teachings hidden within each story. He is an enrolled member of the Lower Elwha Klallam Tribe, and has worked in the fields of Native American education and social services for more than thirty years. His artwork draws from the traditional as well as the contemporary Salish cultures.

Author Bio

Nan McNutt, educator and writer, is the creator of the Northwest Coast Native American Children's Story and Art Series. This educational series includes five books: *The Bentwood Box, The Button Blanket, The Cedar Plank Mask, The Spindle Whorl,* and *The Twined Basket.* Each book is filled with people from different Northwest Coast cultures whose adventures and activities open doors for the reader.

Nan's experiences as a Euro-American teenager growing up in Micronesia made a strong and lasting impact on her. "I was given insight at a very young age to the multifaceted structures and configurations that make up culture and language. I grew up with a great respect and curiosity for cultural differences."

Nan's introduction to Native American people and culture was at the University of Washington, where she developed friendships with Native American students. Since receiving her masters in education (1979), Nan has lived and worked in Native American communities and schools. She has developed instructional materials and leads workshops for teachers in partnership with educators and artists from many Native American communities.

She said, "It is the inspiration from these people, as well as the response from the teachers and students themselves, that motivates me to develop new ways to honor indigenous peoples, their languages, and their cultures."